ALL ABOUT ANIMALS IN THE SEA

All About Blue Whales

Kerrily Sapet

EZ READERS
AN IMPRINT OF MITCHELL LANE PUBLISHERS

CREATING YOUNG NONFICTION READERS

EZ Readers offer nonfiction for beginning readers in PreK through first grade, using simple language, clear illustrations, and engaging facts to build vocabulary and confidence.

TIPS FOR READING NONFICTION WITH BEGINNING READERS

Talk about Nonfiction

Begin by explaining that nonfiction books give us information that is true. The book will be organized around a specific topic or idea, and we may learn new facts through reading.

Look at the Parts

Most nonfiction books have helpful features. Our *EZ Readers* include color photographs and graphic aids, a table of contents, a glossary, and an index. Share the purpose of these features with your reader.

Color Photos and Graphic Aids

A lot of information can be found by "reading" photos, charts, maps, and other graphic aids found within nonfiction texts. Help your reader learn more about the different ways information can be displayed.

Table of Contents

Located at the front of the book, this list shows the big ideas within the text and the page numbers where they can be found.

Glossary

Located at the back of the book, the glossary defines key words and phrases that are related to the topic. These words and phrases can be found in the text in colored type.

Index

Located at the back of the book, an index is an alphabetical list of topics and the page numbers where they can be found.

With a little help and guidance about reading nonfiction, you can feel good about introducing a young reader to the world of *EZ Readers* nonfiction books.

EZ Readers is an imprint of:

Mitchell Lane
PUBLISHERS

2001 SW 31st Avenue
Hallandale, FL 33009
mitchelllanepub.com

First Edition, 2026.

Author: Kerrily Sapet
Editor: Morgan Brody

ISBN 979-8-89260-836-7 (library binding)
ISBN 978-1-58415-001-5 (paperback)
ISBN 979-8-89260-938-8 (ebook)

LC record available at https://lccn.loc.gov/2025950844

Photo credits: Shutterstock, ROMAN RYBALKO, cover, 1, 3, 9, 10, 14, 18; Shutterstock, Northern Owl, cover, 1, 2, 3, 4, 8, 15, 19; Shutterstock, Pong471, cover, 1; Shutterstock, b113, cover, 1; Shutterstock, Sergey Novikov, 5; Alamy, 6–7, Trish Drury / DanitaDelimont.com; Shutterstock, max-Photography, 9, 22; Shutterstock, Wild_and_free_naturephoto, 10–11, 22; Shutterstock, Andrew Sutton, 12–13; Shutterstock, Andrea Izzotti, 14, 22; Shutterstock, Katherine Wallis, 18, 22; Shutterstock, Wirestock Creators, 20, 22; Shutterstock, Chris worldwide, 21, 22; Shutterstock, Goinyk Production, 22; Shutterstock, Gulf MG, 23

Table of Contents

Meeting An Ocean Giant

Imagine you are on a boat. The boat rocks. The sun is warm.

A huge shape rises in the water. A blue whale! You are seeing the biggest animal on Earth. It's longer than three buses and heavier than thirty elephants.

Whale Watching

The whale is blue-gray. It swims with flippers and a wide tail called **flukes**. You only see one whale. Blue whales swim alone or with another whale.

WHALE WOW!

Blue whales look bright blue underwater.

WHALE WOW!
Whales are born with a small amount of hair.

The whale blows a spray of water. It breathes air through a **blowhole**, like you breathe through your nose. Blue whales are not fish. They are **mammals**.

Blue whales are earth's loudest animals. The sounds are too low for you to hear. Other whales hear their groans and moans miles away.

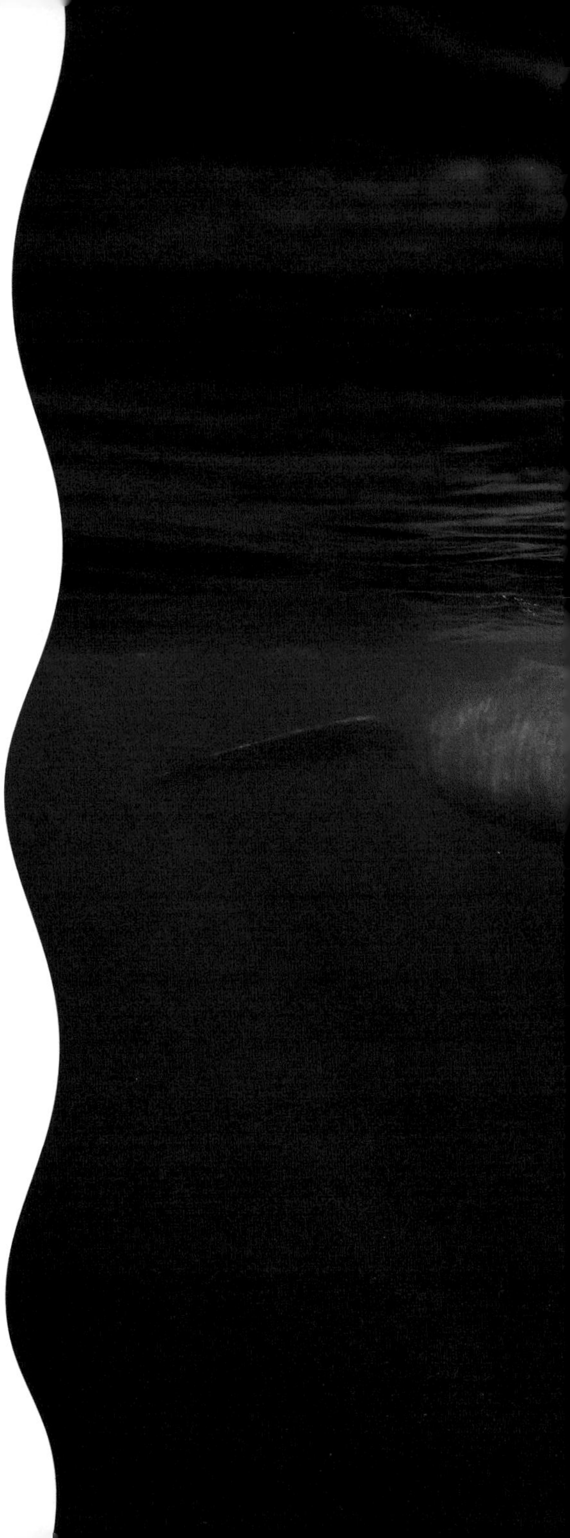

WHALE WOW!

Blue whales eat enough krill to fill 64,000 cereal bowls a day.

Looking for Food

Fish swim near your boat. The whale doesn't eat them. Blue whales eat **krill**—tiny ocean animals. Blue whales have no teeth. They have **baleen**. It's like a comb to trap krill.

You touch the water. It's cold! Blue whales **migrate**. They travel to cold water in summer to find food. They swim to warm water in winter.

Where Do Blue Whales Live?

WHALE WOW!

Whale milk is thick like toothpaste.

Whale Families and the Future

Baby whales are called **calves**. A calf can be as heavy as a car and as long as a van. It gains 200 pounds a day. It drinks milk from its mother.

Blue whales can live 80 to 90 years. Today, only about 15,000 remain. They are gentle with people. Someday you might see a real blue whale.

Parts of a Blue Whale

Flukes
A whale's tail fin is two triangles called flukes.

Blubber
Blubber is thick fat under a whale's skin to keep it warm.

Blowhole
A blowhole is a hole on top of a whale's head. It helps the whale breathe air.

Flipper
A flipper is a flat paddle on a whale's side

Baleen
Baleen hangs from the top of a whale's mouth. It works like a spaghetti strainer to catch krill.

Glossary

baleen (bay-LEEN) plates in a whale's mouth that catch food

blowhole (BLOH-hohl) the hole on top of a whale's head for breathing

calf (kaf) a baby whale

flukes (flooks) a whale's wide tail

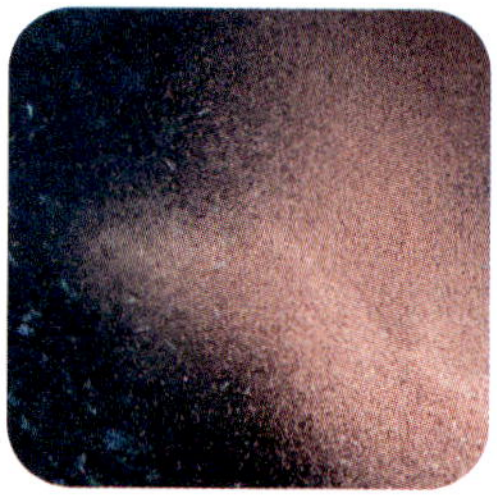

krill (kril) tiny animals that whales eat

mammal (MAM-uhl) an animal that breathes air, has hair, and drinks milk from its mother

migration (my-GRAY-shun) when animals move to find food or warmer water

Quiz

1. **Are blue whales fish?**

   A. Yes   B. No

2. **Do blue whales breathe air?**

   A. Yes   B. No

3. **Do blue whales eat sharks?**

   A. Yes   B. No

4. **Are whale babies called calves?**

   A. Yes   B. No

ANSWER KEY — DO NOT PEEK!

ANSWER KEY:

1. No
2. Yes
3. No
4. Yes

Further Reading

Fenmore, Taylor. *Blue Whales: Nature's Biggest Mammal.* Minneapolis, MN: Lerner Publishing Group, 2024.

Humphrey, Natalie. *Blue Whale: Massive Mammal.* New York, NY: Power Kids Press, 2023.

Pallotta, Jerry. *Who Would Win: Blue Whale vs. Mosquito.* New York, NY: Scholastic, 2023.

On the Internet

Animals A to Z
https://www.montereybayaquarium.org/animals/animals-a-to-z/blue-whale
Learn about blue whales living by California in the summer.

Blue Whale Facts for Kids
https://kids.nationalgeographic.com/animals/mammals/facts/blue-whale
Read more and watch a video about blue whales.

Marine Mammal Sounds
https://www.pmel.noaa.gov/acoustics/whales/sounds/sounds_whales_blue.html
Listen to the sounds blue whales make.

Index

About the Author

Kerrily Sapet has written more than 30 books for kids. She lives near Chicago with her family. When she was eight, she heard whale sounds on a record. She loved the sounds. Sapet has seen beluga whales at the Shedd Aquarium. She likes hearing their whistles, chirps, and clicks. She has never seen a whale in the ocean. Sapet hopes to see one someday.